# ACHIEVING AMAZING (CLIENT) RELATIONSHIPS

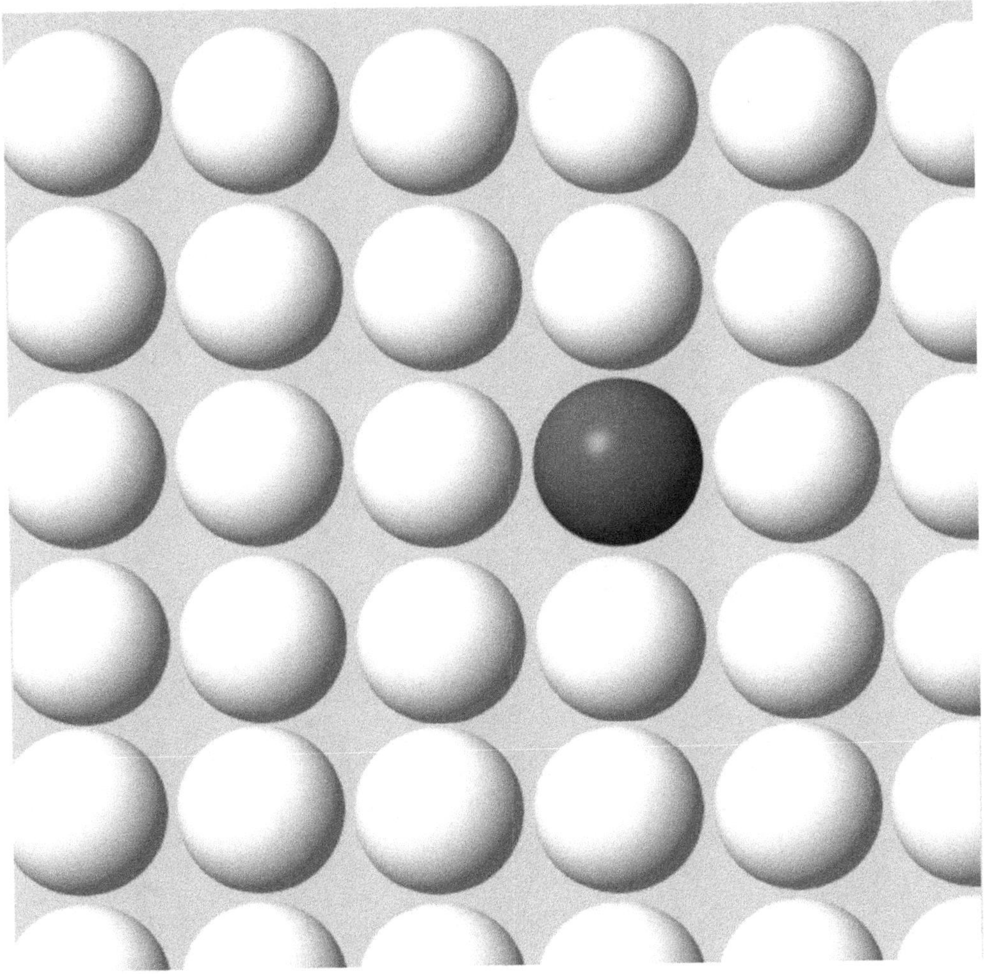

**Frank Gifford, 2022**

Third Edition

For Sharon and our children: Nathaniel, Jeremy and Alexander. And for my dad, who published a book when it was hard.

# PREFACE TO THE THIRD EDITION

Much of the content here is tailored to those in a highly technical field such as penetration testing* who need to have a large amount of interaction with a client. Too many people in these technical disciplines have never been taught "soft" skills. To a paying client, the lack of such skills can come off as abrasive or aloof. This book started as an in-person training and has been used as a guidebook for people I've hired. While the content here is geared towards those in penetration testing and software development, all of it can be used in any field where people are primarily hired for technical skills.

Much like books on weight loss, it's not enough to simply have this book on your bookshelf. There isn't a magic formula or secret sauce contained inside. Instead it's a collection of mindsets which are used as actionable guidelines.

It's been said if you aren't embarrassed by the early versions of a product, you shipped too late. This book is no exception.

---

* Penetration testing is breaking into a computer with the owner's permission. This way flaws can be discovered and fixed before someone does it maliciously.

# TABLE OF CONTENTS

| | |
|---|---|
| WHY? | 1 |
| RESULTS | 3 |
| CHANGING OTHERS | 5 |
| WHO IS YOUR CUSTOMER? | 8 |
| DELIBERATE FLAWS | 14 |
| SOFTWARE DEVELOPMENT MODELS | 17 |
| OBVIOUS TO US IS MAGIC TO OTHERS | 22 |
| DISC PROFILE | 24 |
| HIGH-D | 27 |
| HIGH-I | 28 |
| HIGH-S | 29 |
| HIGH-C | 30 |
| DISC – HALVES 1 | 31 |
| DISC – HALVES 2 | 32 |
| A, B, C PLAYERS | 34 |
| PEOPLE ARE NOT LOGICAL | 38 |
| FAVORITE SUBJECT?  ME! | 40 |
| FOCUSED LISTENING | 45 |

| | |
|---|---:|
| **CORE OF A DISAGREEMENT** | 48 |
| **"IF", "BUT" ARE DEADLY** | 53 |
| **JUDGING BY CATEGORY** | 55 |
| **EFFECTIVE EMAILS** | 59 |
| **TIME MANAGEMENT** | 62 |
| **READOUTS** | 67 |
| **EFFECTIVE PHONE CALLS** | 70 |
| **GROWTH** | 72 |
| **SCENARIOS** | 74 |

# WHY?

*"Begin with the End in Mind." – Stephen R. Covey*

Consulting groups, such as pentesting firms, make money, among other ways, by helping clients find flaws in their computer systems.  Imagine a possible client who is ready to get a penetration test and is deciding between vendors.  This process can take three weeks to three months, and this is for someone who has money in hand and wants to get a pentest.  However, for a repeat client who is doing an annual review, or additional work, this process can be under three weeks start to finish.

Happy customers are repeat customers and cost less to acquire than new customers.  Note we don't want <u>satisfied</u>, we want <u>happy</u>.  Satisfied customers think they got a reasonable value for their money while happy customers get a great deal for their money and say we should be charging more. Less money going out of your company means more money kept.  If you are responsible for happy customers, it's easy for the company to share that wealth with you.

This book won't be about giving up your integrity.  There will be times when a client wants you to change a finding's severity and you will refuse to change it – and they will be happy with your choice.

Many of the examples in this book are from my personal experience having started as a software developer. The concepts presented are chosen so that they will apply to every aspect of your life, regardless of your specific work discipline.

Disclaimer: The content is mine alone including any errors; it's not sanctioned by any past, current or future employer.

I hope you enjoy.

# RESULTS

We live in a capitalist results-based economy. Everything contained in this book is covered by one warning without exception:

**You must produce results that are of high value, high quality and complete.**

You could be the best friend of the Point of Contact. Perhaps you are godparent to their child. You might have even saved their dog's life by giving it CPR. If you turn in a terrible report, the client will fire us and refuse to pay the bill.

Since our company needs to make a profit, a non-paying client is a major problem. First, you still get paid your salary for the time you work for the client. Second, the company has to decide whether to get lawyers involved to force the client to pay the bill. Third, a professional client relationship is damaged since the client will blame the company as a whole. Finally, your time could have been spent working on a different project or in doing useful research.

**High Value:** The findings are useful to a client. They tell the client something they don't already know, or contain a bit of a surprise to the client. Put another way, an attacker would want to know about the finding and could use it.

**High Quality:** Each finding is well written and stands alone as a well thought out explanation of the issue. The spelling of words and overall grammar are correct. Reproduction steps are enough that a client can confirm the finding and verify when it's fixed. Since the programmer who fixes this issue may not know what it is, it needs to be explained in sufficient detail. While we don't need to be pedantic in explaining a finding, it should not require detailed knowledge about penetration testing techniques.

**Complete:** All findings that could have been found are included. If the client were to give the exact same project to a competing company, that company should not find any significant vulnerabilities beyond what is already in our report. While it's fair to argue certain "Low" and "Info" findings might be in a report or not, depending on circumstances, there would be no reason a "Critical" or "High" finding would be missed.

# CHANGING OTHERS

You can't change other people. This seems obvious on a logical level but it's amazing how easily we fall into the trap of trying to change others. A word of note here is that I can't change you either. If you change at all because of what's written here, you will be the one doing the change. I'm only asking that you'll keep an open mind.

A key word here is "**should**". Whenever you hear that word (or its cousins "ought" or "need to"), someone is trying to change someone else. Unless you are in a position to enforce your will, things won't change. Even a parent has trouble making a child change.

"People shouldn't drive so fast."

"The voting public should be better informed."

"You should exercise more."

Trying to change others is futile and is a direct path to unhappiness. You will waste your time and they won't change. On top of that, you will feel frustration as they don't take your amazing advice to heart.

To get around this, you have to take the courageous step of accepting things as they are. Some people will cut you off in traffic, while others will allow you to merge.

That's the nature of reality. You can change yourself completely if you want and that's all that's needed.

Note that I'm not at all implying that you should tolerate bad behavior. You can disagree with improper behavior while accepting that certain people are just rude. This is not some pacifist approach of loving all people. Not everyone deserves your time and attention.

For a client, you will have to accept that in some cases they will disagree with your finding. In extreme cases, they may simply refuse to fix it. There's nothing you can do about this. Keep in mind that a client is paying for two things:

1) *Your expertise in finding security flaws*

2) *Your silence*

Here's an extreme example: On a web assessment you find the robots.txt file includes a directory called "/secret_passwords" and that contains a readable file containing passwords that you confirm are valid. It's a nasty vulnerability and can be trivially fixed. Now suppose the client says that they won't fix it. There's nothing you can do about it. Our non-disclosure agreement with the company prevents you from posting that to any message board or discussing it with anyone outside the company.

They "**should**" fix it, it's an easy fix, and they don't have to do anything.  There's nothing you can do about it*.  Accept it and move on.

---

\* Your only possible recourse is to pass it to higher ups in the company and see if they can help.

# WHO IS YOUR CUSTOMER?

Let's work though a fictional example of Fido, Inc. that makes Wi-Fi enabled pet feeders for families with multiple pets*.

They have a pet feeder designed for houses which have multiple pets. Each animal wears a special collar which is paired with the feeder. When it's time for a specific animal to eat, the appropriate collar plays a special sound. When that animal arrives, a dedicated food bowl is opened up. This way the pet can get different food than others.

If another animal shows up to muscle in and steal food, the dish closes and a robotic arm swings toward the bullying animal and blasts it with a puff of air. Advanced models can give a shock to that collar as well.

Fido, Inc. built all their own robotics and a Wi-Fi stack from scratch. In addition, there's a camera, microphone and speakers so the owners can connect over the web to interact and check on their pets.

---

* Inspired from a real-world product:
www.wirelesswhiskers.com

You've been tasked with doing a full end-to-end penetration test (let's assume that you have all necessary skills and time). This covers every aspect from the hardware to the web – nothing is out of scope.

As part of the initial call, you find out that the reason for such a comprehensive test is Fido, Inc. is looking to sell their company, though they refuse to say who the buying company is. They want to have all of their issues fixed so they can get a premium for selling the company. Let's call that buying company Acquire, Inc.

You'll have all the time and skills you need for this test. Your boss will review the report first and it will be read by the board of directors for both companies (you can assume all the legal paperwork is in place for this sharing). In addition, low level programmers will be reading the report so they can make needed changes.

Here's a diagram of the key players and the report:

**When you are writing the report:**

**who is your customer?**

**Think about this before moving on, consider pros and cons to your answers.**

Despite the diagram, your actual customer is none of those listed entities. It's true that when writing a finding it needs to contain elements that talk to the low-level developer so that it may be fixed. In addition, it needs to be at a high enough level that the board of directors understand the impact if it's not fixed.

Your actual customers are those who will buy and use the product. During the time of the penetration test, you are working side-by-side with the client. You are part of their security team, and you might be the only person on their security team. During this time, you have a "pride of ownership" in the product. You want it to be the best product possible and have no security flaws. The client who is paying for the pentest cares about their product and is asking for our help. It's certainly important that we make the client happy with the presentation of our findings so they feel we are working with them. Ultimately, however, **we serve the customers of our clients**.

It's easy to fall into a mental trap of seeing the work as nothing more than going through some basic checklists as we go through one faceless client after another. Each pentest we do is special to the client and our efforts make the product that much better. No project should be considered insignificant or merely routine. If we treat some work as insignificant, it's easy to overlook findings. Clients have been known to silently get multiple penetration tests from different vendors working on the exact same codebase.

Let's extend this company example another step. Suppose Acquire, Inc. turns out to be a large medical device manufacturer. They love Fido, Inc.'s knowledge of robotics and that they wrote a Wi-Fi stack from scratch. They will keep that stack completely untouched for their future products.

They plan to create a wearable chemotherapy device which would inject micro-doses of a chemical which kills off cancerous cells faster than it kills healthy cells. Instead of a person going to a doctor's office every few days and being massively sick, Acquire, Inc. hopes that giving tiny doses over time will kill the cancer cells and allow that person to go about their life.

A user would pop in a new cartridge every so often, and the device would monitor the patient's vital signs while using robotics to give carefully measured doses. The information is uploaded to the Cloud where a doctor can examine the results and make changes as desired.

It's natural to ask: Would there be any findings in the Wi-Fi stack for the medical device that you didn't find in the pet feeder? They are identical stacks, not one single byte changed.

Arguably, there shouldn't be any differences in the findings between the two. "Unauthorized Attacker Can Dispense Medicine" and "Unauthorized Attacker Can Dispense Food" should only differ in the resulting impact. There shouldn't be an attack that's found in one product that isn't found in the other.  This is the "Complete" part of the "Results" chapter from earlier.

Just because the underlying product feeds pets doesn't mean your efforts should be any less comprehensive.  You never know where your tested code will end up.  Whatever you choose to do, do it with all your attention and focus.  At the end of a test, you should feel that you found everything that was in your power to find.

Paraphrasing from Simon Sinek's, "Start with Why"*

> *Two bricklayers are working on a building site. You go to the first bricklayer and ask him what he's doing. He responds that he's laying bricks. You go to the second bricklayer and ask him the same question.*
>
> *He responds "I'm building a cathedral".*

---

* http://www.becomingwhoyouare.net/start-with-why/

# DELIBERATE FLAWS

Clients don't put in deliberate flaws in to their code. Sometimes we act as if the client is incompetent or is malicious. The reality is that no matter how important security is to us, it's just not that important to everyone else.

In every business book, security is never discussed, unless it's what a company specifically sells. It's always "features" and "time to market" which drives activity. Security is an afterthought. Even in the more recent data breaches, companies rely on insurance and offers of free credit monitoring as a way to make up for their fumbles.

I worked at a company that did deep packet inspection of network traffic. The goal was to reassemble TCP flows and examine what was being sent, such as a malicious PDF file. If we found an attack, it would automatically be blocked along with that source IP address. During the job interview, I asked what happened if an attacker presented a massive number of complex files which were malicious. The machine certainly couldn't keep up, so what happens?

The answer surprised me: Although it was a setting controlled by the customer, the vast majority of the time the customer would allow the attack traffic to go through. I was horrified. From a customer's perspective, they assumed they had plenty of other protections and the loss of business related bandwidth was much worse for them than possible malware.

Many businesses have competitors who are perhaps just a month behind them in development.  In a world dominated by being on the first page of a Google search, "time to market" overwhelms everything else.  A recent concept is a Minimal Viable Product, namely a product that's just barely usable but is in the hands of a customer quickly.  Features will be added if there are customers who are willing to pay.  If no one wants to buy the product in the first place, then the time spent is much less than a full product.

In addition, bugs are truly hard to find.  Back in my time as a product developer, it was common to spend days trying to reproduce a bug.  Programs which run in parallel on multiple threads and multiple cores while sharing data can crash in the most bizarre manner.  They are so vexing that the programmers think that the compiler or even the computer chips might be at fault.

With all of this effort, there is no time for a client to put in a deliberate flaw.  Sometimes we act as if the client is being malicious.  In reality, they borrowed some code online and it works for their normal use case.  Maybe they've documented it as a possible flaw and then promise to get back to it.  Then they just forget to revisit it, or the programmers leave the company for a better opportunity.

The company is trying to get the product to work and get it out the door into the hands of paying customers. The common use cases need to be solved. They allow file uploads so customers can load an avatar for a social media related site. They verify that the extension is a supported image type and then they move on to the next issue.

All the while, the boss is stopping by every day wondering when the work will be completed. When an employee walks in or out of the building, the boss makes a dramatic showing of checking their watch.

Our clients are not putting in deliberate bugs into their code. While some of the buggy behavior we see might be bizarre, it's a lack of proper knowledge, not malice.

# SOFTWARE DEVELOPMENT MODELS

There are two primary software development models that have been developed over time. One is Waterfall, the other is Agile. Each has a particular time when it's appropriate and it typically depends on the complexity or impact of the resulting product.

**Waterfall**

This is characterized by a "top-down" approach, typically for large projects which involve several unrelated components owned by different companies. An air-traffic control system, or software running a space station are good examples. This was developed in the early 1970s and is often used for cases where the downside risk is significant, such as loss of human life. By providing guarantees at a high layer, the program can be "proved" to behave in a correct and deterministic manner.

In this model, a committee is formed to start with high level requirements and break them down. At some point this can be given to various companies and they eventually break it down to the code. Typically, you hear about software contracts, such as a guarantee that a software event will be processed in no more than 100ms from when it was sent.

Eventually the different pieces are put together and everything magically works.

**Agile**

This is a more recent concept which allows a Minimal Viable Product approach to programming. The programming team works in "sprints", usually two to four week increments. At the beginning of each sprint, the programmers commit to the features they will incorporate for that round. This is driven by complexity since some features might be more difficult to implement than others, even though externally it may appear otherwise, such as letting a user dynamically choose a color for a page which is currently hard coded.

For each iteration, the software gets closer and closer to the outcome the customer wants and everything just magically works.

## Reality

Although the two above are the primary software development models, there is a third one which is reality. It starts off as one of the two above and then breaks down. Here's a diagram:

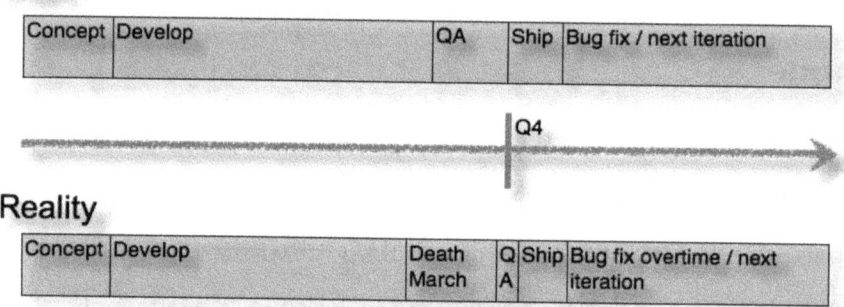

Figure 4: Desired Development vs Actual Development

The client promised a customer, the financial market, or a Venture Capitalist that a product would be shipped by a certain time. In the example above, the company promises that a program will be ready by their fourth quarter (Q4). This way they can get paid for the entire quarter and investors like money that can be made all quarter.

Time is allocated for all the major pieces such as development and quality assurance. Everyone agrees it's a good plan*. Then the plan is put in motion. Unfortunately, code is hard to write and bugs harder to squash. Things take longer than expected. People get sick or go on vacation. Worse yet, higher-ups will state what features are required for various sprints (which violates the Agile model).

Since time is running short, and the company made an external commitment on the shipping date, the quality assurance time gets squeezed. To be sure, the QA department is busy during this time testing pieces, but they can't do end-to-end testing.

Towards the end, there are 80-hour workweeks and no vacation time. "Can you reschedule your root canal for after we ship?" Ultimately, the product ships, a little late but not terribly so. Critical bugs are fixed over the next little bit in 80-hour workweeks until things calm down.

Upper management promises that they've learned a great deal about the process and none of this will happen again. There's an optional reorganization with some programmers leaving or joining the company. Lather, rinse, repeat. I've seen this in every programming project I've been in or observed from a distance. These issues are

---

* Actually, it's a very aggressive plan. You can't tell your boss the truth, otherwise you'll be accused of sandbagging or spending too much time on social media. "Yes, boss! We will make that happen!"

not a problem with the models – they are a deliberate, but well-meaning, violation of the models. In all of this, there's no time for a client to find and fix tricky security flaws, let alone put in a deliberate flaw.

# OBVIOUS TO US IS MAGIC TO OTHERS

Sometimes flaws are obvious. As a pentester, if you find a file upload capability on a website, you already know a dozen things you will try to use to break it. If you ever find a SQL string being built by string concatenation, you already have the basis for a finding, even if you never find a specific exploit.

But for our clients, these ideas seem non-intuitive. In fact, they get the feeling that we are performing magic. When a client starts, "How did you think to ..." - that's an indication you performed a magic trick.

We might, in fact, be so good at these intuitive jumps that we forget a time before when we didn't know about them. It's almost as if we knew about these attacks from the moment of our birth, even though it's just a checklist that we cross off on our way to completing a pentest.

*Figure 5: Drawing from my brother*

My brother, Sean, is eleven years younger than me and, as a child, he quickly drew the above one day. He was unable to explain how he did it since he was already in the level of "Unconscious Competence". Any individual line he drew, it just seemed like it belonged at a particular place.

It's like that for us and going through findings. While we may use checklists, they are more of a reminder to not overlook anything instead of a how-to. We instinctively notice when an error web page discloses the web server version. From there we know to look up for known vulnerabilities. But none of this is obvious to our clients, not even the ones who are technically savvy.

# DISC PROFILE

"Communication is what the listener does." – Mark Horstman

The DiSC profile* is an amazing tool to understand how people naturally communicate. By understanding how people give and receive information, you can tailor your communication in a way that makes it easy on them. Our first two children are twins, and I've seen this first hand. When they were toddlers, they would carry on detailed back and forth conversations, which all sounded like "Ba-DA!" over and over. Then one would locate a toy for another and it was clear they had a communication system they understood.

Some people want a "big picture" view of an issue. Others want all the gory details. Other people seem to care that pointing out a security flaw might hurt someone's feelings. Using the wrong communication style for that person will increase friction. If you start describing a particular software flaw in great detail, a listener might get very irritated if all they care about is whether it's easy to fix. Conversely, a different listener might want detailed proof that a flaw can actually be exploited before making a fix.

---

* https://discprofile.com/ - And, yes, it's "DiSC" with a lowercase 'i'.

Unlike other "personality tests", you can quickly find out other people's styles, since it's based on observable behaviors. More to the point, we aren't trying to get inside someone's head to see why they act a particular way. We want to find out how people communicate when they aren't thinking about their communication. Knowing this means we can tailor our communication style to be more in line with theirs. There is certainly work to make this change and it won't happen quickly. It's hampered even more when our emotions rise up. Over time, you'll learn how to communicate in a way that's easier for the listener.

When covering these styles, it's important to keep in mind that there isn't a "right" profile. Each has a set of strengths and weaknesses to them. No communication style is better than the other. You can get your specific profile for $30*.

Here's a quick overview before diving in:

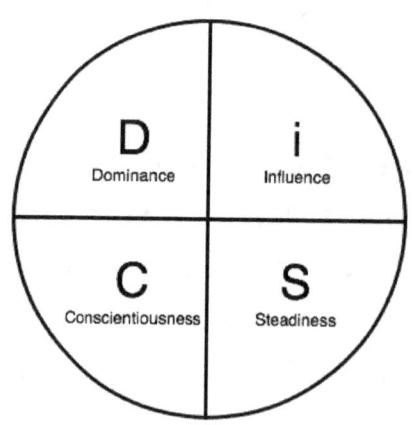

**Range is 1-7 each**

**Larger is "More"**

---

\* https://www.manager-tools.com/products/mtdisc-profile

The measurement will give you a set of four digits, ranged from 1 to 7, which will be in the order for "D", "i", "S", and "C", going clockwise around the above circle. A larger digit means more of that trait, smaller means less. In my case, I'm a: 2-1-4-7, which corresponds to a little "D", practically no "i", some "S" and a high amount of "C", or simply a "High-C".

It's easier to cover the four main types with some stereotypes so they are easier to remember. Then I'll cover a neat trick to quickly figuring out a person's style and then how you work with that.

By observing how a person communicates, you'll get a quick sense for their style. It's worth pointing out that it won't be a single piece of data, but rather a collection of this data which you will use.

Remember that the communication style is the way we prefer to communicate by default. We can change this depending on who we talk to and it's very common for more senior people in a company to have mastered the different styles and will communicate differently with different people. Whether conscious or not, they have learned how to match their style to the other person in a conversation. Reading people like that may be tricky and you may need several observations to be sure.

# HIGH-D

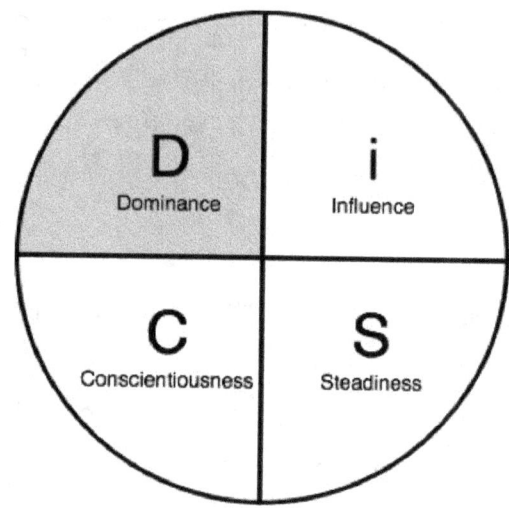

The High-D has a vision for the future and you will implement it. Your opinion is irrelevant. They are a fast thinker and way ahead of you. If you ask an opinion, they'll give it to you direct and won't sugar-coat it.

Behavior characteristics: Focused on tasks, interrupts, active, loud, big gestures, talks about larger picture, looks you in the eye when talking, glances at emails, one word responses to them.

Weaknesses as seen by others: Rude, abrupt, interrupts, harsh, uncaring, doesn't care about details, doesn't fully read emails.

Perfect job: Drill sergeant

Terrible job: Grief counselor

# HIGH-I

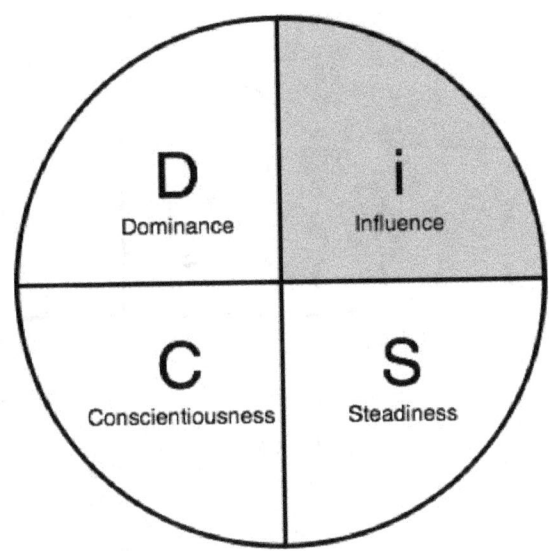

A High-I can sell anything to anyone. Everyone is a "new best friend," even while in a checkout lane at a grocery store.

Behavior characteristics: Focused on people, loud, listens, active, talks about larger picture.

Weaknesses as seen by others: unfocused, too happy, too chatty, no attention to details, unreliable for deadlines.

Perfect job: Sales

Terrible job: Tax accountant

# HIGH-S

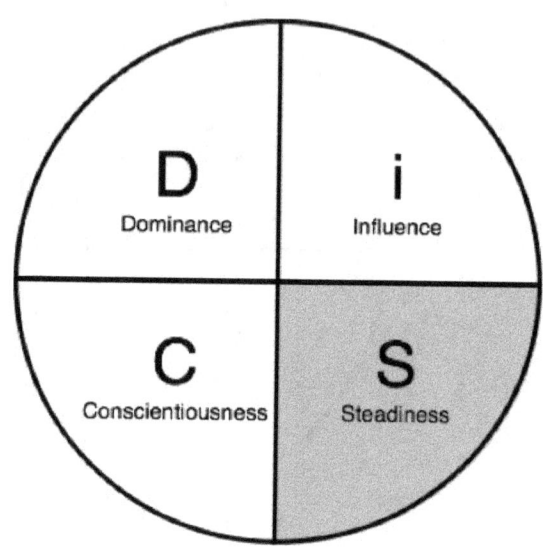

    A High-S puts other people first and is a great listener. In addition, a High-S can understand and give advice for complex people problems.

    Behavior characteristics: Quiet, listens, soft spoken, small gestures, talks about details, thinks before speaking.

    Weaknesses as seen by others: Emotional, cares less about business priorities than people, shy, won't stand up for themselves.

    Perfect job: Kindergarten Teacher

    Terrible job: Bouncer at a bar

# HIGH-C

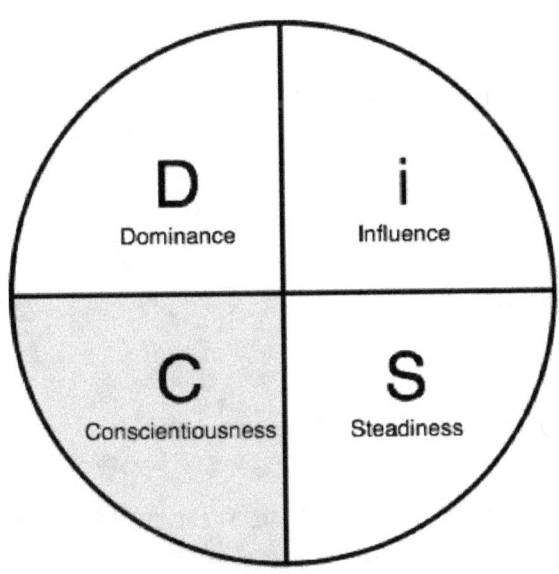

High-C's are detail focused, and can keep those details in their head all at the same time.

Behavior characteristics: Focused on tasks, thinks before talking, pauses while talking, small gestures.

Weaknesses as seen by others: cold, pedantic, judgmental, no personality, no eye contact, lengthy emails.

Perfect job: Computer programmer

Terrible job: Door-to-door sales

# DISC – HALVES 1

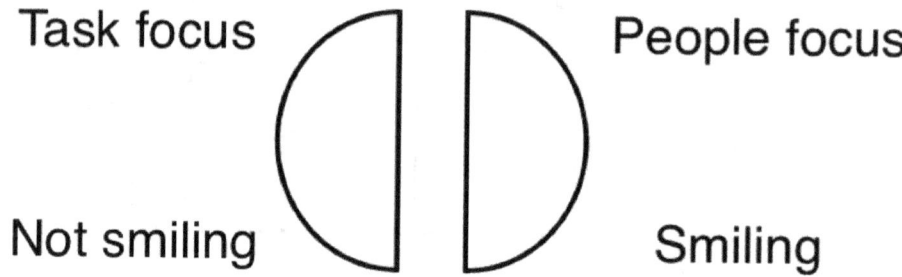

Task focus — People focus
Not smiling — Smiling

    Instead of trying to remember the four types and their combinations, it's easier to think about the two sets of hemispheres.  In the above left vs. right, we can quickly gauge a person by the observed behavior.  The first is to find out if they talk about work or people.  Another is whether they naturally smile or don't.  Remember that you're looking for a collection of behaviors, not just one data point.

    Also, you aren't looking for the reason for the behavior.  You'll never be sure what's inside a person's head and it won't matter anyway.  When you see a majority of behaviors pointing one way, that will indicate the proper hemisphere.  The way to remember this pair is "task" vs "people".

# DISC – HALVES 2

Active, Loud, Big picture, Large gestures

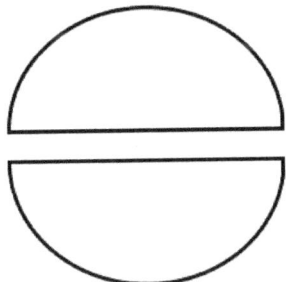

Thinking, Quiet, Details, Small gestures

In this case, the way to remember the difference with this pair is "Active" vs. "Passive". The upper half are loud, large gestures and strong eye contact. What they choose to talk about will often be in the future. The lower half are focused on the present and in details. They will often think a moment before speaking and their gestures will be smaller, not leaving the boundaries of their torso.

Matching another's style can be tricky at first. Adjusting what you talk about (people vs. task), your volume, your eye contact and the depth of your subject (big picture vs. details) will go an amazingly long way to matching them.

As mentioned earlier, none of these styles is "right" or "wrong". When you know a person's style, you won't be caught off guard by their behavior. For example, if you are a High-S and you are talking with a High-D, you know they interrupt as part of their style. It's not a personal attack and they aren't uncaring or trying to hurt your feelings.

# A, B, C PLAYERS

Along with DiSC, it's useful to understand the concept of A, B and C players. These indicate a person's mindset and understanding them will allow you to know how to react. Generally, these correspond to great, good and poor.

### A Player

This person is described by others as "great". They love what they do, are dedicated and take pride in everything they do. Further, they are always learning and while they know a lot, they know the limits of their knowledge. They take criticism of their code well since they realize the code isn't perfect. In addition, they will thank you for the bugs you found.

### B Player

Described as "good" or "competent". They like what they do and learn new skills if their manager requires it. Unfortunately, they suffer from Imposter Syndrome*. Most people are B players. When you give them a finding, they get annoyed at themselves for the flaw.

### C Player

---

* The feeling that people will discover the limits of your knowledge and judge for not knowing everything, regardless of your depth.

Described as a poor performer, or "used to be good". This person has retired in place and has no desire to learn. A common phrase heard from a C player is "That's just the way I am" or "That's not my job". When you give a C player a finding, they worry about being fired.

Interestingly, we can change between these levels our entire lives. We might leave college with some good knowledge and a desire to learn and we work our way into being experts and A players. After some time goes by others realize that all we care about is the vesting of our stock options and we're now comfortably a C player. Usually this process takes several years to go between levels.

Let's look at a common problem: a client pushes back on a finding. Instead of blindly responding to this or defending your position, take a moment to understand what's going on from the perspective of an A, B or C player.

Why would an A player complain about a finding? Only if it's technically inaccurate. Perhaps you marked a possible finding but it doesn't really apply in the client's environment. Would an A player ever complain that a finding was marked as a "High" when they think it would have been better as a "Medium"? Even a former pentester would separate your findings from what they will do in the company. At best you'll get, "You've marked this as a High, but internally it's pretty low priority and we'll get to it later."

B players will worry if there's a lot of findings and may try to get one or two reduced. But if there's just one or two major findings, they will let it go. Mostly they are concerned about the extra work that will be needed to make the required changes.

C players are worried about one thing only: getting fired. The findings will point out the shortcuts they implemented. They've probably already had a couple bad reviews with their manager and have been put on notice that they could be fired at any time. These people will complain about several findings, especially ones that are severe. What will mystify you is the ease of some of the fixes. It will be as simple as updating a third-party library.

It's important to note that just because a client complains about a finding doesn't mean they are automatically a C player. Consider what they are arguing. Is it just the severity? Is it about the ease which an attacker could make the attack?

If the client promised to fix everything you found, would the rating really matter to you? There are times when you need to stay with a rating because it's our opinion of a finding, this is especially true for boilerplate findings. But for findings you created from scratch, you have some leeway. However, keep in mind some effects for the future. The client may come to expect fiddling of the levels.

How do you handle an A player pushback?  You won't need to.  If they disagree with it, it will be something you can add to a "Customer Response" section.  Essentially the only thing they will say is that your finding is really a false positive, i.e. the reported version number indicating a nasty vulnerability was actually fully patched and the version number wasn't updated on purpose.  They have an IDS looking for hackers trying to attack that apparently vulnerable service.

B player pushback: Acknowledge the time required to fix it.  Not in a way that you feel sorry for them, but in a manner of "Good thing we found this before a bad actor did".  Also, you can have "This is a common flaw that we see all the time and it's easy to overlook."

C player pushback: Indirectly remind them that the flaws would be an instant firing, "Yeah that was a nasty bug, good thing we found it since the effects would be devastating."  If it's an easy fix, fixate on that as well making it clear that they can fix the flaw and still get drunk at the bar on time.

# PEOPLE ARE NOT LOGICAL

All of our decisions seem logical and completely rational. We can justify everything we do with logic. When looking at others, it seems they are being illogical. The reality is that everyone is illogical. We all make decisions for emotional reasons and then our conscious brain comes up with logic after the fact.

Once you accept this fact as reality, then the behavior and decisions of others start to make sense. People have their own reasons for their choices, and those reasons make sense to them at the time. It's why people smoke cigarettes which cannot be defended by any logical argument.

When a company has poorly written code, you don't know the sequence of events that happened to get to that point. Likely, they were understaffed and had an aggressive schedule with several required features. Perhaps the programmers were pushed to develop code which was just outside their capability. Programmers join and leave a company at different times. The design decisions for a program might have been made by people who since left the company. A security flaw might have existed from the beginning. Since the code works, from a business perspective, and doesn't crash, it's not given another look until we are hired.

It's important to assume that people mean well. They didn't mean to have a flaw in their code. When we make a mistake, we like to talk about our intent and how we were trying to do the right thing. "Sorry I'm late for the meeting, I had a flat tire." Make a conscious effort to accept that other people aren't malicious and they mean well.

"We judge ourselves by our intentions and others by their behavior." - Stephen M.R. Covey

# FAVORITE SUBJECT? ME!

"Most people do not listen with the intent to understand; they listen with the intent to reply." – Stephen R. Covey

A person's favorite subject: themselves. They're an expert too since they've known the subject their entire life. Many conversations are littered with the words "I" and "me". Or we use someone else's conversation to then talk about something we know a lot about and get to show off our intelligence and depth of knowledge*. Focused and active listening are not natural to us, and it is the single biggest thing we can do in improving any relationship.

When a person talks about themselves incessantly, it bothers us since we aren't part of that conversation. It's a one-way brain dump. They could be saying those exact words to anyone else on the planet and we get the feeling that we aren't important to the talker. We do this naturally as children and it takes effort to recognize it, or a trusted friend to point it out.

Ask open-ended questions to allow the other person to take over the conversation. Even better are questions where you don't know the answer and it would give some

---

* Here I am giving talks and writing books about it. Aren't I clever?

insight. A great conversation should have a back-and-forth exchange of ideas and both sides should be happier because of it.

To have great conversations, the topics should also be positive in nature, or be required for a better future. Too many of the "conversations" we see in the news are two people with completely different views or interpretations of an event who don't listen to each other and interrupt at every opportunity.

Remembering a person's name is a fantastic way to show that you like them and you care. Granted, it's difficult to remember names when you are meeting several people at once for the first time. That's natural since there's an overwhelming amount of information to process. There are a couple keys to easily remembering names. The first is to forgive yourself if you've forgotten a name and say to them, "I'm sorry, I've forgotten your name."

The second is to understand that the way to remember a name is to give the other person your full attention as if they are the most important person in the room. Get out of your head about what you will say next. It's the "listening to respond" that trips us up in remembering names. We aren't in the moment, we're actually a couple of seconds into the future. When something happens in the present, such as hearing a name, it's easy to let that information drift off into the noise.

Staying in the present means literally this instant. Not one second forward or backward in time. Thoughts such as "Why did I say that?" or "I need to mention the rock climbing I did" are both somewhere other than the present and what is being said gets ignored. Stay in the present.

When you introduce yourself, remember that while you know who you are, others have no idea. If you say your first and last name together, have a slight pause between the names. This gives the other person a chance to process the first name. If you have an uncommon name, slow down and enunciate it*. "Hi Jason, my name is 'Ra – Ha – Nick'."

Aside from a person's name, what else is important to them? Their family. If you are a manager and you don't know the names of your direct report's spouse or children, how good could your relationship possibly be? What if you need to ask for overtime or work on last minute travel? You'll have to fall back to role power to get things done. While this is effective, it's only good in the immediate term. Every such use of role power will harm a relationship. It's similar to a parent's response of "Because I said so."

Now instead imagine that, as a manager, you know all about their children and the karate belts they just

---

* You're going to do it anyway on the third or fourth attempt when they lean in and ask you to repeat it, you may as well do it up front.

earned. When the children visit the office, you put out your hand to one and say, "Hi Janice, how are you today?" How would your direct report rate your relationship? If there is a job offer for a slight increase in salary, how likely would it be accepted?

A great way to practice remembering people's names is when going to a restaurant. The server will come by with a prepared speech starting with their name and immediately diving into selling high-margin drinks or appetizers. In this case, the name is said as a mere formality.

When the food arrives, a simple, "Thanks, Martha" will feel awkward at first but will make a difference. Sometimes a manager will be making the rounds and will ask how everything is. Imagine a response of: "The food's good and Martha has been taking great care of us." Your response will be so rare and can easily help get her an immediate raise. If you've forgotten the server's name during this process, it's fine. It's so common and you're just another faceless person. You can try again next time.

Phone calls with a client are usually relatively short and stay on topic. If there's some waiting time for everyone to arrive, allow the client to talk about themselves or their company if they want. This would be a good time to mention something positive about their code, if it's sincere and above average. "This was a fun project to work on and your team was really helpful when answering our questions."

When you have in-person meetings and on-site work, you'll have more time for non-work discussions. Letting the client talk for 70% of your conversation will work wonders. Asking open ended questions are a great way to keep the conversation going, though avoid starting with "why".

Questions starting with "why" are too accusatory and imply that the opposite decision was the better choice. It's similar to a parent asking, "Why did you run in the house?" There's an inherent negative tone and judgement to it.

# FOCUSED LISTENING

Focused listening means that our attention is with the other person and nowhere else. On an obvious physical level, it means we aren't checking our phone while others are talking. We look at them, we nod or shake our head to indicate we are following along. When others walk nearby, we don't look at other people. We certainly don't start talking to that other person, regardless of how much we need to talk to them.

Less obvious is that we aren't thinking about what we will say next. Our attention isn't about some grocery item we need to pick up on the way home. If we aren't focused on the other person, it will be obvious as we get a distant vacant look on our face. Pretty soon we've missed a chunk of the conversation and they know it.

Active listening is being able to understand the words and meaning behind what is being said. It isn't the ability to repeat a conversation word-for-word. When a person believes that you are truly listening, they will appreciate you even more. If, however, you aren't listening with focus, they will feel that you don't care about them as a person. Imagine that you go to your boss to talk about your child who has gotten severely ill and needs to be hospitalized. During this conversation, your boss is typing away on the computer and looking at the screen saying, "Uh huh... Yep..." Then, as you take a deep breath to steady yourself your boss says, "Yeah, go take the time you need." Is this focused, active listening? Was checking email helpful or harmful to your relationship?

Another key is to understand if the other person is asking for advice or just venting. It took me years to learn this lesson with my wife. She would talk about a few things which were bothering her and I would offer up useful suggestions which, surprisingly, seemed to irritate her. The more I solved problems for her, the worse it got. Eventually, I asked if she wanted me to let her vent or if she was asking for a solution. It turns out that sometimes she was venting. So now, when she says, "I need to vent," I let her get out everything she wants and I don't offer any suggestions. At the end, she's much happier, even though no problems were solved from my perspective.

We also look for ways to ask open-ended questions and questions based on curiosity. However, avoid questions starting with "Why", since they come over as accusatory. When the other person in a conversation believes that you understand their point of view, they will feel appreciated. If you interrupt an explanation, you don't understand. Too many times the reason we interrupt is that we think we understand what is being asked and the other person has talked long enough. For the High-D and High-C people, this is normal and they won't be offended. However, for a High-I or High-S, it's exceptionally rude.  When you aren't completely sure of someone's style, don't interrupt.

Part of active listening is being able to understand and restate what the other person is saying.  When you've restated their issue and they say, "That's right!" - they are saying that you understand them.  However, if during a discussion they say, "You're right!" - that's them giving in to your will power and they don't agree with you and they are out of energy to fight.

# CORE OF A DISAGREEMENT

We get into various disagreements all the time. This is made worse by our 24-hour news cycle when they will have two people on with opposing views who talk over each other and refuse to listen. Even a simple reading of a comment thread in social media quickly breaks down to name calling by people who clearly did not read the previous posts. Something as simple as a basic corporate email can turn into a series of snarky back and forth comments such as this gem:

> *Good point. Once something has been done once, literally no one should ever look into that topic again. That's why I just write to memory straight on the network stack, rather than using netcat, since the network stack already works, why use a newer tool that makes that easier?*

An argument gets extended because you aren't listening. This is worse over email without any body language, facial expressions or tone of voice. Too often we assume the worst when we read an email and then hastily rush off a response. Text messages are even worse with their brevity and instant response.

This next sentence may cause you some discomfort and it's important that you digest it.  A person has a right to have an <u>opinion</u> that is their own, even if you disagree with it.  That opinion is an extension of the person, so if you invalidate or misstate an opinion, you invalidate the person.  Deliberately taking a person's opinion and misstating it by going to an extreme will be taken as a fight.

A coworker and I were discussing Uber at some length.  He discussed, in significant detail, his dislike for Uber and that he much preferred their competitor, Lyft.  He spent some time listing Uber's corporate behavior around sexual harassment, the lack of being able to give a tip via Uber and that Uber drivers just don't get paid enough once you factor in all the use of the vehicles.  He was quite opinionated and passionate.

Personally, I despise renting a car and I'd much prefer to use a service such as Uber.  From my experience, every Uber driver has been great and I got to my destination just fine.  Even the drivers who had no personality still did a great job of driving.

It would have been easy for me to "disagree" with my coworker's opinion by stating my experiences and implying that's he's wrong to think the way he does.  That would be the wrong approach.  The correct way is to first acknowledge the other person's opinion without agreeing with it.  Remember the "Changing Others" chapter from earlier?  You aren't going to change other's opinion.  He's allowed to have an opinion that's different than yours.

Instead, use phrases that indicate curiosity and that you are picking up some information or are seeing the world differently.  "I hadn't heard about that, I'll have to do some research."  "Really, I had no idea."  And it's at this point you'd state your opinion.

For the High-C person, when they describe their opinion, they want to be very exact.  This is why us High-Cs can talk incessantly about a topic.  It's not enough for us to state a generic opinion of "I like cheese."  It has to be fleshed out, nuanced and every combination explained.

Interrupting the stating of an opinion implies that you already know what their opinion is.  Even if the person has been going on for five minutes, they haven't fully told you their opinion yet.  As a High-D or High-I, this can be infuriating as they ramble on and you've already got the idea they "don't like Uber".  If it's an opinion you disagree with in a very general sense, it's even more aggravating while waiting for a chance to speak.  Interrupting them is dismissive and you'll notice that they will come back to finishing up their statement when they start talking again.  Let them finish, since they eventually will, you can start with something such as, "You've clearly given this some thought" or "I wouldn't have guessed this was this important to you, that's interesting."

The way to take the above opinion and turn it into a fight is to take their argument to an extreme: "WELL! If you HATE Uber so much, why don't you quit your job and picket in front of their offices every day?" Or, "If you LOVE Uber so much, why don't you drive for them instead of working here?"

Interestingly, many lively discussions are actually about minute differences between opinions. When you examine the subject from a distance, you'll often find that they aren't that far apart. People can quickly get lost in the nuance, since that difference is what sets us apart from others who have an otherwise similar opinion.

Regardless of the differences of opinion, you aren't going to change the other person. If you want to add your opinion to the discussion, you'll need to keep that in mind. Acknowledging the other person's opinion, even if you disagree with it, will go a long way in your relationship. If you want any hope of changing their mind, you'll need to acknowledge their opinion first as an extension of themselves. Then you present your information with something like, "Have you thought about..." or "It seems like ... would be pretty important."

Be on the lookout for the word, "Should". If part of their opinion involves changing other people, don't bother being a part of that discussion. Sadly, this happens a great deal whenever politics comes up for discussion. As soon as anything political comes up, people interrupt with their opinion and the word "should" starts flying around.

No matter how any of those conversations go, absolutely nothing will get done and no opinions will change.

For a client, this difference of opinion is often about the severity of a finding.  Some clients have security as a distant thought.  While a client company purchased a pentest, the people on a readout call may not be the ones who want a test and they may see us as an impediment to getting work done.  It's our opinion that using a web certificate with an MD5 hash is bad practice, and it's this client's opinion that it's a non-issue.  Since you aren't going to change the client's opinion, there's no sense in wasting time on it.  Definitely keep it in the report and defend your finding, just don't be surprised when a client isn't swayed by your ten-minute nuanced explanation.

# "IF", "BUT" ARE DEADLY

Email communication is hard enough. All the body language and tone of voice are lost. Extra care has to be used to be sure that a misunderstanding doesn't spiral out of control. Here's an actual quote from an email.

> *Thanks for your input if you would have read the email you would have seen where I said "<client> DOES NOT want us reporting on site" and hence payed for an extra week of reporting ;)*

Despite there being a "thanks for your input" and a "wink emoticon" at the end, the "if you would have read the email" puts a particularly nasty edge to what should have been a basic email. Instead, a much more effective email would be:

> *Thanks for your input. <client> doesn't want us reporting on site and paid for an extra week of reporting to make up for it.*

In everyday conversations, the "if" statement when applied to someone's state of mind almost always implies something negative.

"I'm sorry _if_ my actions offended you." "_If_ you found that offensive, I'm sorry." The "if" can be implied too: "I can see how you _might_ see that as offensive." Or: "Those who I _may_ have harmed, I'm very sorry."

Using "but" implies a negative, typically meaning that you disagree with the premise. "Your work is good _but_ you need more concrete examples." "I like that idea _but_ we don't have a budget." "I like your product _but_ you have a major SQL injection bug."

Instead of "but", use the word "and". It's a little odd at first, and you'll be using it in no time. So now the statements are "Your work is good and you need more concrete examples." "I like that idea and we don't have a budget." "I like your product and you have a major SQL injection bug." Now these statements have an entirely different meaning.

A great tip to help your kids play well with others is to not let them use "no" or "yes, but". Instead, use the improvisation technique of "yes, and". Before it was: "Blizzard throws a snowball." "No, he makes an icicle sword." Pretty soon the kids aren't playing well. After the change, it's: "Blizzard throws a snowball." "And he pulls out an icicle sword!"

# JUDGING BY CATEGORY

There is a trap in thinking about people as a category that they are in, and it's in the same vein as prejudice, literally meaning to "pre-judge." A simple example around "Millennials" will make this clear.

If you are under the age of thirty and working for our company, your parents would consider you to be a "success". By any objective measurement, you are in a growth industry doing highly skilled work which will be in demand for a very long time. But does that mean that everyone your age is a success? Certainly not. Do you know of anyone under the age of thirty who is a bum, a criminal, or is otherwise a drag on society?

The reality is that "Millennials" today are no different than those in their twenties back in the 1960s. They use the latest technology that they can afford, want to work for a company that cares about their ideas, want an opportunity for advancement, and want to do something to make the world better.

When we assume that a person's ambition, mindset or behavior is driven by the group they are in, we are prejudging them and not treating them as an individual. This is true regardless of the category: Millennials, Baby

Boomers, females, males, Koreans, color-blind, Catholic, wealthy... Everyone wants and <u>deserves</u> to be treated as an individual.

Here's a thought experiment. You're told that you have a new coworker who is joining the company later today. You're told she is a 22-year-old who just graduated college. What can you tell about her?

Does she have any pets? If so, a cat or a dog?

Is she married?

Does she have kids? Does she want kids?

During her free time does she prefer to curl up with a book or climb a hill?

Is she better at Windows or Unix?

What is her race?

What is her DiSC profile?

The logical answer is that we know nothing other than her sex, age, education and that's she driven enough to be hired by us. Beyond that, we don't know anything. For managers, this is especially difficult since it means that you will have to get to know her as an individual and not as a "female" or a "millennial".

The reason we group people into categories is twofold. First, it's a simplification trick used by our brains. There's so much data to process and our brain is constantly trying to find shortcuts. When that shortcut works, we stick with it. The particular fallacy here is "confirmation bias". Namely, we group people and then when we see behavior confirming our bias, we remember that. Items that go against our bias are conveniently ignored.

The second reason is our news media. It's easy for the media to group people together based on the behavior of one person. Person X does something bad; person X is a member of group Y; therefore, all members of group Y are bad. This is especially terrible during national elections. "How will the <group> turnout affect the election?" Substitute various groups in the previous sentence to see how easy it is to categorize and judge.

The trap is to follow a bias, <u>even if it's statistically valid</u>, and apply it to a specific person. When you are dealing with an individual, treat that person accordingly, and not their group membership. To take a fictional example, let's suppose that we have a large scientifically valid study that applies to our newest hire. From that study, 90% of the people in that group love dark chocolate. Should you assume that she loves dark chocolate? You might gamble that way, but there would be a 10% chance that you would be wrong. Imagine starting off a conversation with, "According to this scientific study, you love dark chocolate." If she's in that 10% who doesn't, you've permanently damaged a relationship. If she's in the 90% who does, you've <u>also</u> permanently damaged it. No one wants to be judged by a category, whether it's something in their control or not.

How do you manage a "millennial"? That's the wrong question. The right one is "How do you manage an individual?" Treat her like the individual she is. Ask questions to find out what drives her. Find out what's important to her and the limits of her knowledge. Figure out what gaps there are in her knowledge and help her come up with a plan to fill those gaps. Have measurable deliverables to know when she's achieved the milestones.

How do you talk to a Baby Boomer client when you are on site? Talk to the individual without regard to age and without assuming you know anything about them first.

# EFFECTIVE EMAILS

We use emails and phone calls for the vast majority of our daily conversations in the company as well as with clients. Effective use of emails can make a huge difference in your perception. Since there is no body language or tone of voice, the reader is left to interpret the message. Our brains are wired to look for danger much more than pleasure*. An email that has even the slightest bit of harshness to it gets magnified out of proportion.

Added to that is the problem of making assumptions about what the other person knows or meant. We forget that other people don't have the same knowledge as us in all situations. Even when we talk about a project we are on together, I may have a critical piece of information that you don't know. I can interpret your email in light of this knowledge I possess that you don't. The results are usually disastrous (see the "If" chapter for an example).

A way to get around this is to assume positive intent – namely that the other person doesn't have some piece of information. They aren't looking to have a fight. If you have a desire to fire off a snarky email involving this hidden knowledge, pause for a moment. Is it possible that

---

* You can thank our distant ancestors who noticed rustling grass indicating a predator was approaching.

they don't know this data?  If they didn't know it (or forgot it), would the email make more sense?

Part of your job is to make the other person's job easier.  Just because you send an email doesn't mean it or the attachments will be read.  To make an email effective for the listener, use the Bottom Line Up Front ("BLUF") technique.  This will tell the reader right away what you want them to do.  When examined from the DiSC profiles, the Ds and Is won't read more than a sentence or two of the email.  They are too busy or distracted.  While the Cs and Ss will read it, they will appreciate knowing what you are asking for in the first place.

Avoid an either-or question.  "Should I do A or B?" is a terrible question since a High-D will answer "yes".  Instead, ask "Should we have pizza for the candidate lunch?  Sushi would be a good alternative."  Now an answer of "yes" is clear.

When you send email to a distribution list and want people to write you "off list", mail the message to yourself and use the BCC option instead.  The "Blind Carbon Copy" sends the email to everyone on the list, but when the reader presses "Reply-All", it will only go to you.

An inbox is for unread messages.  Once processed, put them elsewhere as needed.  A full inbox is not a badge of honor, it means you are ignoring conversations.  Ignoring conversations means you don't value the other person.  You can create Inbox rules to automatically file distribution list emails, or ones where you are in the "CC" list as opposed the "To" list.

Turn off pop up notifications. You don't need a window to pop up along with a bouncing icon and a sound playing just because a coworker sends an email that they will be working from home. Every such distraction pulls you away from your task at hand. Those can all be turned off from your email client.

When you receive an email that makes you want to fire off a snippy response, **stop**. Really stop and think about whether the other person intended to say something that was trying to be uncaring. Is it possible they are simply expressing an opinion about something and you have a different opinion? Emails are forever and saying something directly rude cannot easily be taken back. It's worth that thinking time first.

# TIME MANAGEMENT

People consider themselves to be overwhelmingly busy*. The reality is that people are, in fact, a lot less busy than they think. Most of the time it's a problem of managing priorities. A good way to prove this is with a time analysis created by Peter Drucker, a well-known author in business management, especially for the higher executive levels. You would instruct a secretary to follow you throughout the day and write down everything that you did, to the minute. After a week, you have enough data to then compare your work time to your priorities. Arguably, the top priority should get most of your time. The data will show otherwise.

For most of us without a secretary to follow us around, the variation of this is to use a random timer and a notebook. The timer will go off in random intervals, roughly ten minutes apart. Then, whatever you are doing in that instant when the timer goes off, write down the time to the nearest minute and the activity. This includes getting a cup of coffee, having a cigarette, talking with a colleague about a bug they are solving, meeting with a client, using the bathroom, or taking a phone call with your spouse.

---

* If you tell your manager you aren't swamped with work, you'll be given more until you are.

Do this for a couple of weeks and then write down all the activities which appear and their counts. Surprisingly, most people never reach more than fifty percent of their time spent on true work. A forty-hour week might actually be twenty hours of productivity. In addition, it's likely that when you match those items up against your priorities, you'll find they don't line up the way you would like. A great book to help with this is, "Getting Things Done" by David Allen.

It may seem odd to include time management in a book about client relationships. Remember that the absolute top requirement is results for the client. By being efficient with your time, you will have more time available for the results to be complete and well researched.

Much like focused listening, there's focused work. When you find something that may be a possible finding, track it down. Document the finding completely in the reporting document and then move on to the next item. Anything which helps you stay focused is fine, such as marking off blocks of time on your calendar, or even things such as the "Pomodoro Technique". Ultimately, not being distracted will be a huge help.

In addition, stay with one item at a time. It's too easy for us to find a few findings which we would normally mark as a Low or Medium and to not put them in the report right away. After all, we are typically looking for Critical and High vulnerabilities. Towards the end of the reporting time, we go back and look at the overlooked findings.  If there's a finding you would report, do so as soon as you encounter it.  You will be documenting this anyway, so you may as well do it while it's fresh in your head.  Then you get the added bonus of being able to pass that finding on to the reviewers much earlier in the gig.

Spend a little of your time at the end of a gig to think about automation or checklists.  Were there limits to your knowledge during that testing?  If so, make the time to go learn what you need.

A common thing I see consultants doing wrong is trying to find every finding in the client's code, and then trying to rush a report on the last day.  Sometimes that's pouring through incomplete notes, a jumble of screen shots, or trying to recall that one oddball finding you meant to document but forgot to write down.  Then they work late hours on a Friday, or work over a weekend to get the report completed and delivered to the client before the start of Monday.

Instead, as you discover a finding, add it to the report along with any screenshots and supporting documentation.  Include reproduction steps as needed and have the finding ready for a review.  If it's complete, mark it as ready for review and let the next person in the chain review it.  At this point, you're done with the finding and can go on to find the next flaw and the finding is now out of your head.  Any reviews can be done at their convenience.

Amazingly, sometimes the clients are watching what we do and they fix the flaws as we discover them.  There is nothing inherently wrong with this approach since they don't want to leave bugs lying around.  If you forgot to grab a screenshot or the exact wording of an error message, you may not get another chance to do so.

Sections of the report, such as the Executive Summary, can be written in pieces throughout the engagement.  The boilerplate information can be put in along with some key findings as you go along.

Another reason for the documenting as you go is that it's absolutely not fair to your reviewer to dump twenty findings at 3:30PM on a Friday and state that you need to deliver the report to the client by 5PM.

Every time you partially work on a finding and set it aside to work on another, there's a "task switching" cost.  Each transition has a time and stress cost which adds up.  Then when going back to the original, there's a cost to get your brain back into the spot where you left off.  Did you have a screenshot?  Do you need to crop it, or was that already done?  Are there reproduction steps which are easy for the client?  What was that thing you wanted to check next?

There's a hidden benefit to doing each finding to completion: most of the "task switching" goes away and adds up to give you more spare time.  That spare time can now be given to the client in the form of looking for low-probability but high-yield findings. These would be the "moonshot" type of attacks. Perhaps a third-party library they use has a zero-day attack and now you have time to investigate that.

Here's proof you can't multitask*:

1. Find a partner.

2. With your right hand, prepare for a thumb-war.

3. While you are engaging in a thumb war, your left hands will simultaneously play continual games of rock-paper-scissors. Enjoy the challenge!

---

* https://www.weareteachers.com/proving-the-myth-of-multitasking-with-a-simple-experiment/

# READOUTS

This is the "Your baby is ugly" meeting. Often this is the one time when the client realizes their code isn't as good as they thought. Perhaps they expected a few flaws to be in the code, but not this collection. The primary reason is in case the report needs clarifications, or for those people who didn't take the time to read the report. This last part might come as a surprise. Remember from the DiSC profile that High-Ds and High-Is won't read the report all the way through. With everyone believing they are too busy, this meeting may be the first time they are reading the report at all.

Keep in mind two critical mindsets: You serve the customer, not the client (don't say that out loud!); You sit on the same side of the table as the client as part of their security team.

Use phrases that discus the findings dispassionately, i.e. "The code", not "Your code". When referring to the code or findings, use "It", not "You". An example would be, "The code builds SQL strings by concatenation and we were able to construct a query as shown in the reproduction steps. This allowed us to add an administrative user into the database."

> "**For the love of God, don't ever read a paragraph of text to your client word-for-word. They've actually passed a remedial school and are able to read just fine on their own. Summarize and highlight a couple of important points if needed.**"
>
> **- Frank Gifford**

When I do this as a presentation in a room, I put up a giant slide with this quote exactly like this taking up the entire screen and I don't say a word. Then I wait until people have stopped reading it and are looking at me. Then I ask how many people were expecting me to read that quote to them word for word. Many hands will go up. It's a natural thing to do this and everyone admits feeling weird when they expect someone to start reading to them.

Your client's time is valuable and they are able to read. Give a summary, highlight what's important and then move on. Sometimes it's just boilerplate in case they read the report a year from now. It's OK to say so!

Some findings might be low individually, but as a group might be used for a significant breakthrough and your time on the call can be spent walking the client through this. For example, one web finding allows an arbitrary reading of files owned by the web user. Another finding might allow the listing of directory contents. Combining the two and knowledge of the web server, you could now read a session specific file containing cookies of a logged in administrator and impersonate that user. Two otherwise medium findings are turned into a significant exploit. Even though you may have made an appendix explaining this, it's still worth calling attention to it.

If you are having a readout in person at the client's site, try to physically sit so you don't have the client entirely on one side of a table and your company on the other side. Often, the client will bring in more people than you've worked with during the engagement. Ideally, sit next to someone you haven't met, put your hand out and introduce yourself. Then engage in a conversation while waiting for the meeting to start. This is still worth doing even if they end up being the lowest level employee in the company.

Ultimately, you're not having the readout to prove you are right, but to help the client understand. They may never have heard of an XXE attack and you may be giving them a quick understanding of it. Others they may know about and overlooked or otherwise discounted.

Having reproduction steps will go a long way to proving the attack. In addition, if the reproduction steps can be done from a command line, they would then have a way to add this to their test automation to be sure the problem stays fixed forever.

# EFFECTIVE PHONE CALLS

Phone conversations are second only to email for a way to be in contact with our clients. Although the client can get your tone of voice, other nuances such as body language and facial expressions are lost. In addition, phone lines tend to be noisy which make communication more difficult.

If you are by yourself, pick up the handset instead of using the speaker phone. The quality of your voice will sound a great deal richer.

While on a call, use intense focus to stay with the call. This is not a time for email. If you are such a peripheral person that you don't need to be there, then you shouldn't be a part of it to start. Assuming that you need to be on the call, stay focused on what's going on. To help this process, don't use a mute button. Too often we lapse into using a mute button and then have a side conversation, or drift off to catch up on email. Then we notice the droning on the phone has stopped and there's a pause and then our name is spoken. We fumble with the mute button and try a weak, "I'm sorry you cut out, could you repeat that?" It's a complete lie and the client knows it. They do it all the time too.

One of the more dangerous inventions is the mute button. Maybe you reached out to press it and you miss, perhaps hitting it lightly or a different button altogether. Now you think you're muted but you aren't, and you start with a side conversation or perhaps you bad-mouth the client. When the client hears you call them a bunch of "clue-bags" or worse, there's no unwinding and apologizing for that. Even if the mute button works, sometimes you press the wrong button and hang up the phone.

While going through the content, be sure to slow down a little and have some pauses. Let the client interrupt since they may have some nuanced questions for you. There are also plenty of digital delays in telephone circuits, even today. The communication isn't quite at the speed of light and people are more likely to appear to interrupt each other. Let the client interrupt. They are paying for the call.

Sometimes you need to call a client and you reach their voice mail. When leaving a message, leave your name and phone number first. Then leave your message, and then leave your name and number again. When you say digits, slow down and have slight pauses so they can be written down. The reason for leaving the name and number in the beginning is that many voice mail systems will only play a message from the start. Having it at the end again will allow them to verify that they have the correct number before calling back.

# GROWTH

While this collection is less about how to get along with people, it overlaps enough that it needs to be included.

- *Doing something rarely is stressful and you're (initially) bad at it. If you did "Christmas" every month, you'd get really good.*

- *When you can, sit with people you don't know. Why would you go to an all-hands and only sit with your immediate coworkers?*

- *If you would like to eventually be good at something (i.e. public speaking), make small steps in that direction. Volunteer for in-office micro-talks for example.*

- *Publicly commit to taking training or certifications which you know are important. Commit to when you would take the exam.*

- *Have fun and look for non-sarcastic humor.*

- *Don't bad mouth the client, even if they deserve it. Absolutely never while at their site, and not when you are on the phone. Even if they never know, your attitude won't match your actions or words and they can detect that.*

- *Focus on what you are <u>for</u>, not what you are <u>against</u>.*
- *The brain accepts all talk as truth - stick to positive talk.*
- *If you make a mistake, apologize and don't bother to explain your intention.*
- *Forgive other people for their mistakes, they meant well and they aren't doing things on purpose to make your life difficult.*
- *Work is not complete until it's reported as complete.*
- *Never surprise people with bad news.*
- *Fix problems you encounter, especially if they are small.*
- *"Not my job" will stall your career.*
- *Forgive yourself for not knowing enough yet.*

# SCENARIOS

Throughout a workshop, I mix in a series of miniature role-playing scenarios which could happen during a readout call. One person is the pentester, the other is the client. I hand them each a small snippet of paper with their information and we do a back-and-forth. Each scenario takes under a minute and we can then discuss ways the wording could be better, etc. I've included most of that list here for completeness.

After the background is presented to the group on an overhead slide, either the client or pentester goes first depending on the order listed. When I do this in person, the client doesn't get to see the pentester notes, nor does the pentester get to see the client notes.

**Wi-Fi WEP in use**

Background: A company Wi-Fi network was found using WEP encryption which was easily broken with aircrack-ng.

Client: We use encryption and the WEP key should have been unguessable.

Pentester: Walk client through how the tool works and how easy it is for an attacker, including action from a distance by using easily purchased antennas.

## Binary not using ASLR

Background: A daemon process used in a company's product is not compiled with ASLR protection that's available on the underlying operating system. No buffer overflows were discovered in the time provided.

Pentester: Explain finding.

Client: Doesn't matter if we haven't seen any buffer overflows yet.


## NFS Leaks PII

Background: An internal pentest discovered an NFS share which is readable to everyone who can connect to it. Backup tar balls were discovered which contain PII such as credit card numbers and driver's license pictures.

Client: It's not writable and it is internal, what's the big deal?

Pentester: How this was discovered and what an attacker can do with this, and how to lock it down.


## Outdated Wordpress

Background: A bank has an online message board running WordPress with a vulnerable plugin that allows posting and attributing the post to any other user in the system. The finding is marked as a HIGH.

Client: The message board is on a completely different set of computers from the online bank, not even the same subnet and there are strong firewalls to prevent any communication between the networks. This report will go to the board of directors and anything of a HIGH or above will be a problem because of compliance issues. **Goal: Reduce the finding to a LOW.**

Pentester: You created this finding from scratch. You picked HIGH after discussion with a couple coworkers. The fix appears to be a simple upgrade to the plugin.

## Missing AV on upload

Background: The client has a web application with a document upload capability for authenticated users who are world-wide. They accept several document types such as Microsoft Word and PDF. However, they don't do any virus scanning of uploaded documents. The benign "EICAR" string was used to verify the behavior.

Client: When recreating the above finding, your desktop anti-virus software deleted the offending document when you downloaded it, so there's no reason for this finding. **Goal: Remove from the report. Alternatively have "Client Response" portion include the fact that up-to-date anti-virus software is in use.**

Pentester: Why is this a problem? Why is client solution incomplete?

## Internal Default Apache Tomcat

Background: An internal pentest discovered an Apache Tomcat server with default credentials in use. The machine was ultimately taken over, though no pivoting was possible in the time provided.

Client: It's not internet facing, and it's an internal server, no big deal.

Pentester: Why is this a problem?


## Susceptible to phishing

Background: A phishing email campaign was a "password strength checker". Captured passwords were used against a separately captured password hash database to determine a couple harder passwords.

Client: **Read the following out loud:** "Who are these people so we can punish them?"

Pentester: Your response?

## Ports open to internet

Background: An external pentest found some unnecessary ports open to the internet. Not much of value was found on those ports and appear to be temporary web servers, none were exploited.

Client: Nothing of value here, so who cares and why bother reporting?

Pentester: What is your response to the client?


## Too many domain admins

Background: Some 50 domain admins were found. Best practice is that there should just be a few of them and these accounts should not be used for day-to-day work.

Pentester starts: Explain the finding and then best practice.

Client - **Read the following out loud:** "We have work to do and we don't live in the world of make-believe. Some of these admins were from companies we acquired and politically we can't just take away their access."

## Weak password policy

Background: Password hashes were retrieved for Foo Bar, Inc. via a different finding. 20% of these passwords were cracked in the time provided and most were lowercase with digits. Often had names of people or company name so would be "guessable", three passwords were "foobar2020".

Client: If we just locked down the password hashes from the other finding, isn't that enough?

Pentester: What is your response to the client?


## strncpy defined as unsafe

Background: Code review shows that the "strncpy" and related functions are #defined to be the unsafe "strcpy" versions. No actual buffer overflows were found in practice, so this is an INFO.

Pentester: Describe the finding.

Client: If there's no overflows anywhere, what does it matter?

## Widely deployed root password

Background: Client's downloadable package has a fixed root password in /etc/shadow which is never changed. It's clear that it's the same for every customer. The hash was not broken in the time provided.

Pentester: Describe better practice

Client: Previous pentest from other companies pointed this out and none of them cracked it either. Only a couple people in the entire company know the password and not even the managers. You won't change it.


## XSS on document description

Background: With a web application, an attacker can upload a document and put in XSS code into the document description which uses markdown. Although the site sanitized '<' characters, the following string was accepted for a markdown hyperlink:"[foo](javascript:alert(String.fromCharCode(88, ..."

Client: I thought that escaping characters would be enough.

Pentester: Your response?

## LM hashing in use

Background: An internal pentest found Windows LM password hashing to be in use. All passwords of 14 characters or less were quickly broken.

Client: But 14 characters can't be brute forced.

Pentester (In the class, I pick someone who is knowledgeable about Windows LM password hashing): Explain the weakness of LM and how it's actually directly breakable.


## Unsecured network printer

Background: A multiple-function printer on the internal network has default admin credentials. Using those, the domain credentials for the printer are revealed. These credentials were used in other findings leading to a full system-wide compromise.

Pentester: Explain how even minor security flaws may lead to a larger compromise. Give ideas for how such an attack can be stopped.

Client: What can be done to detect this issue before it happens? Pentester could mention to you: Logging of admin access to the printer and attempts to use known default credentials.

www.ingramcontent.com/pod-product-compliance
Lightning Source LLC
Chambersburg PA
CBHW070301220526
45465CB00004B/1693